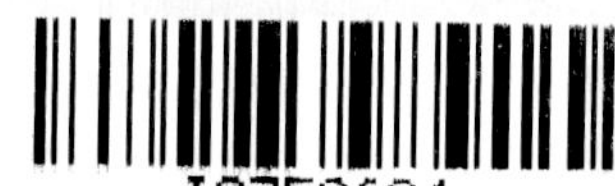

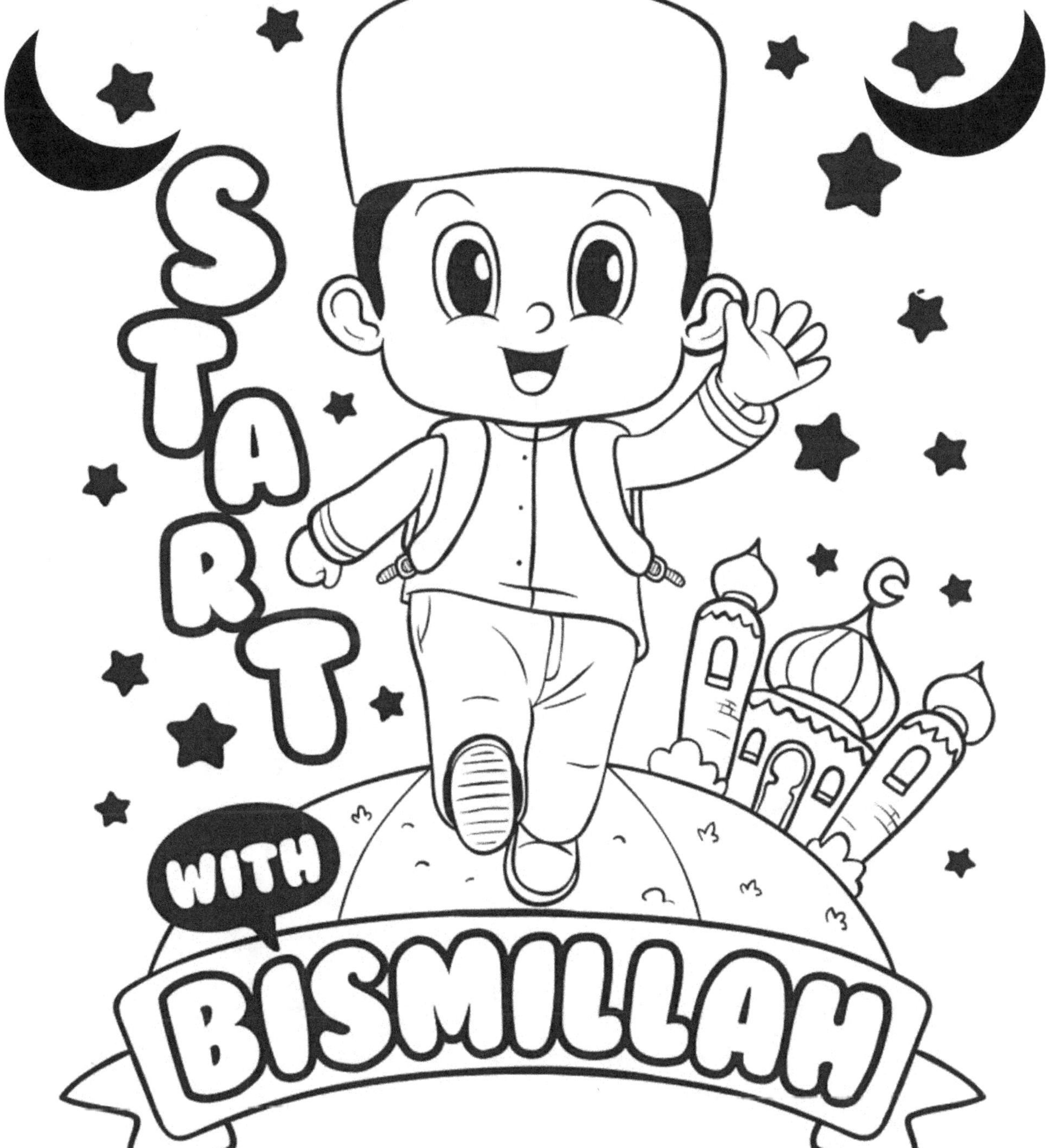

START WITH BISMILLAH

THIS BOOK BELONG TO....

....

....

....

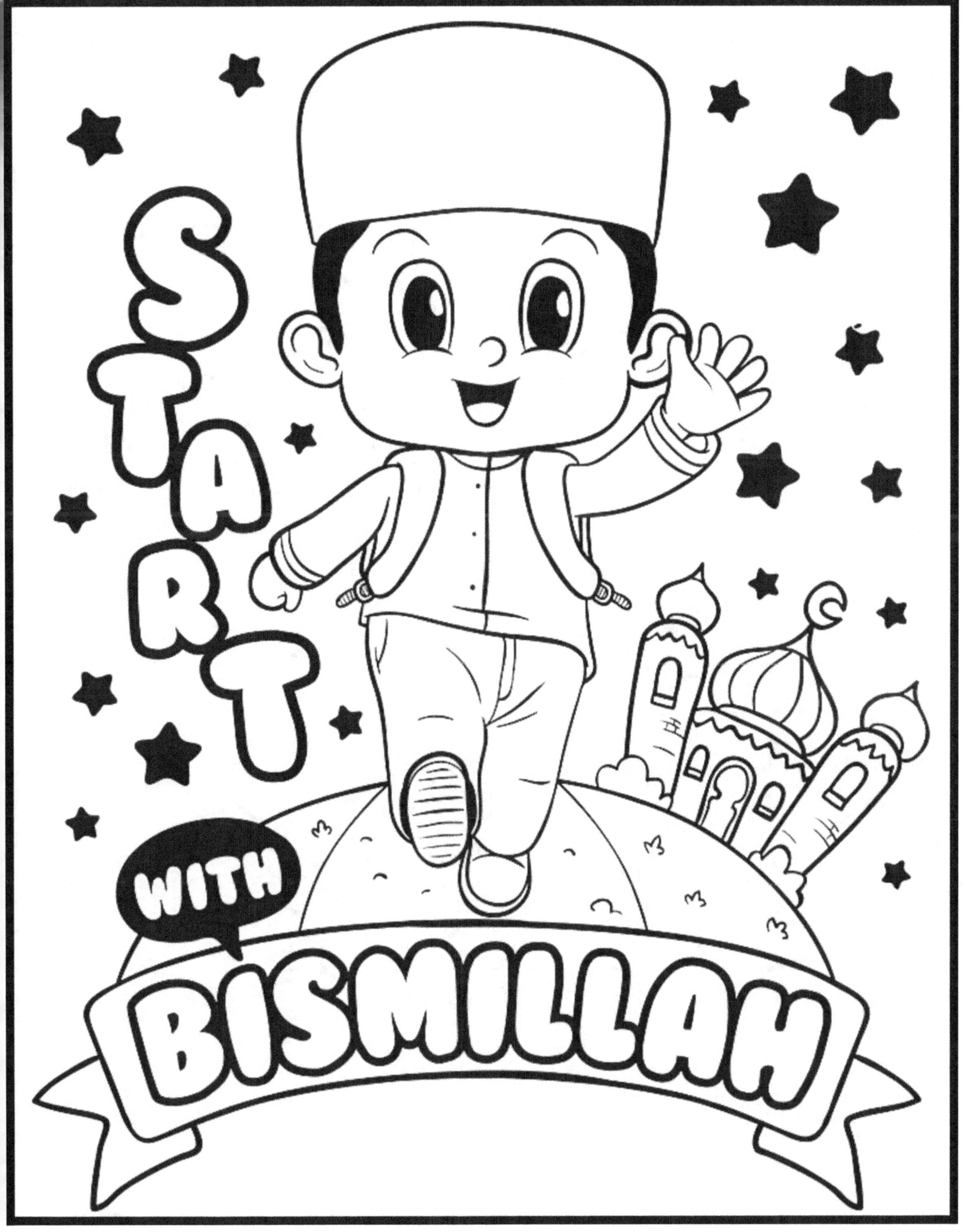

START
WITH
BISMILLAH

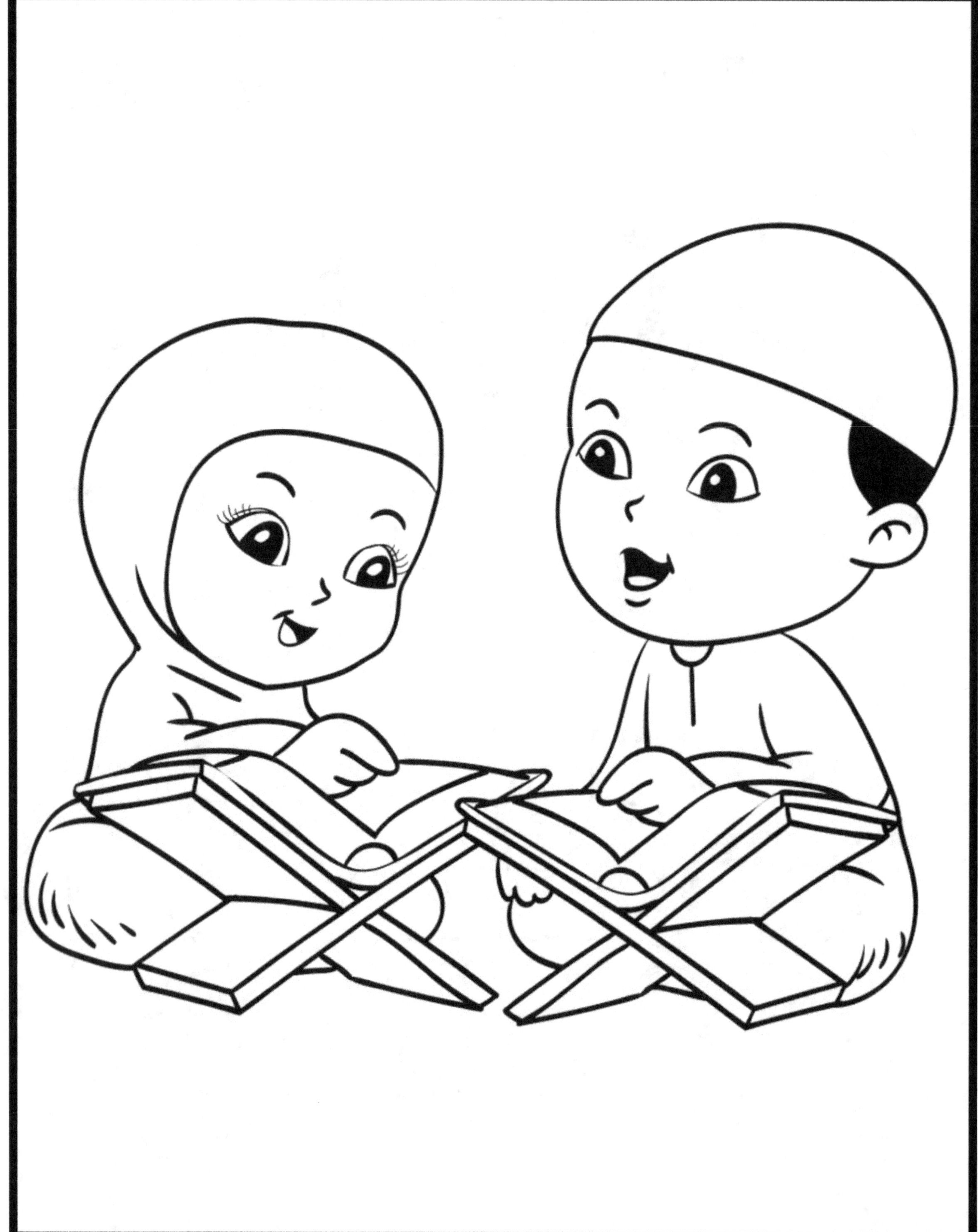

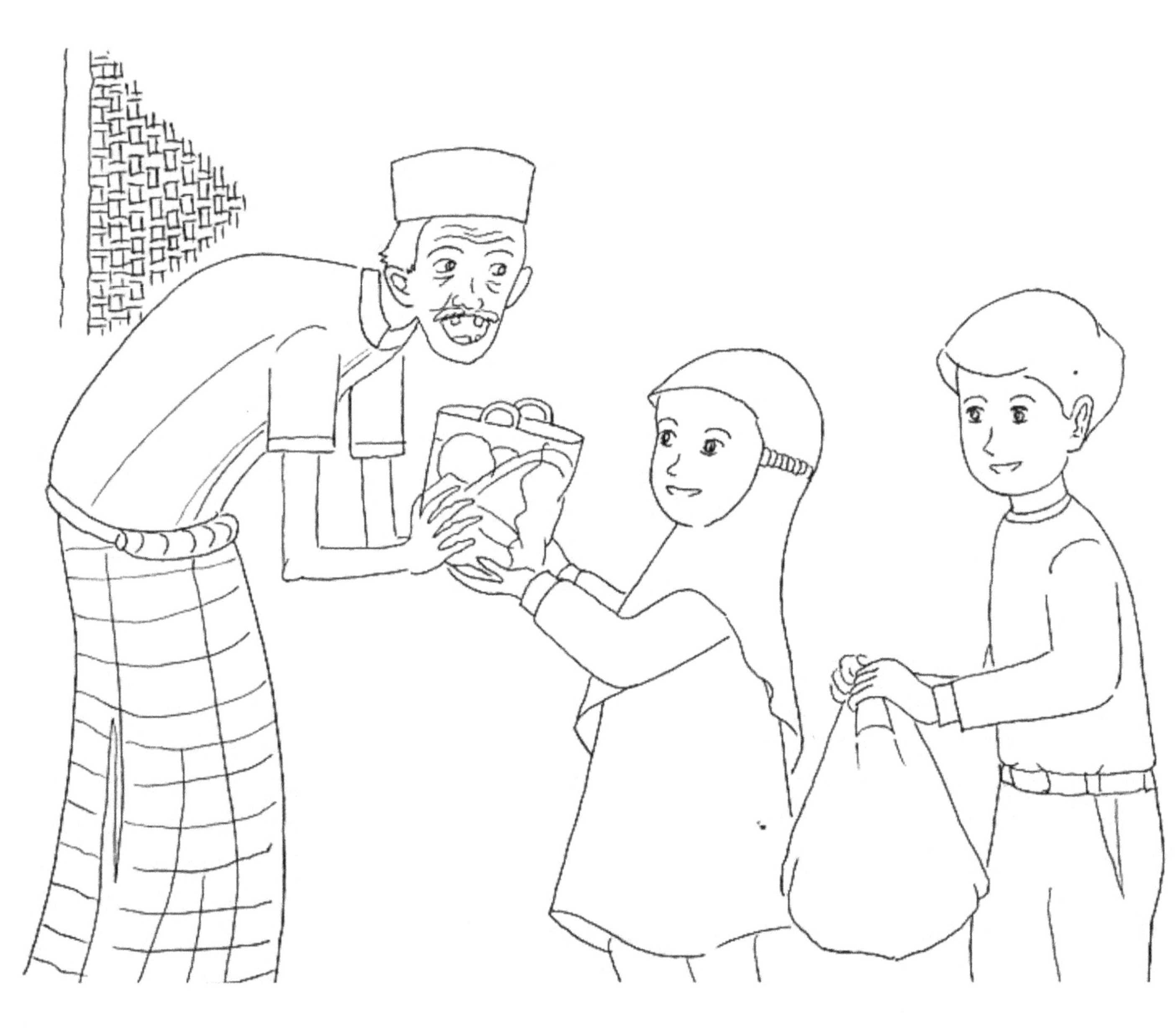

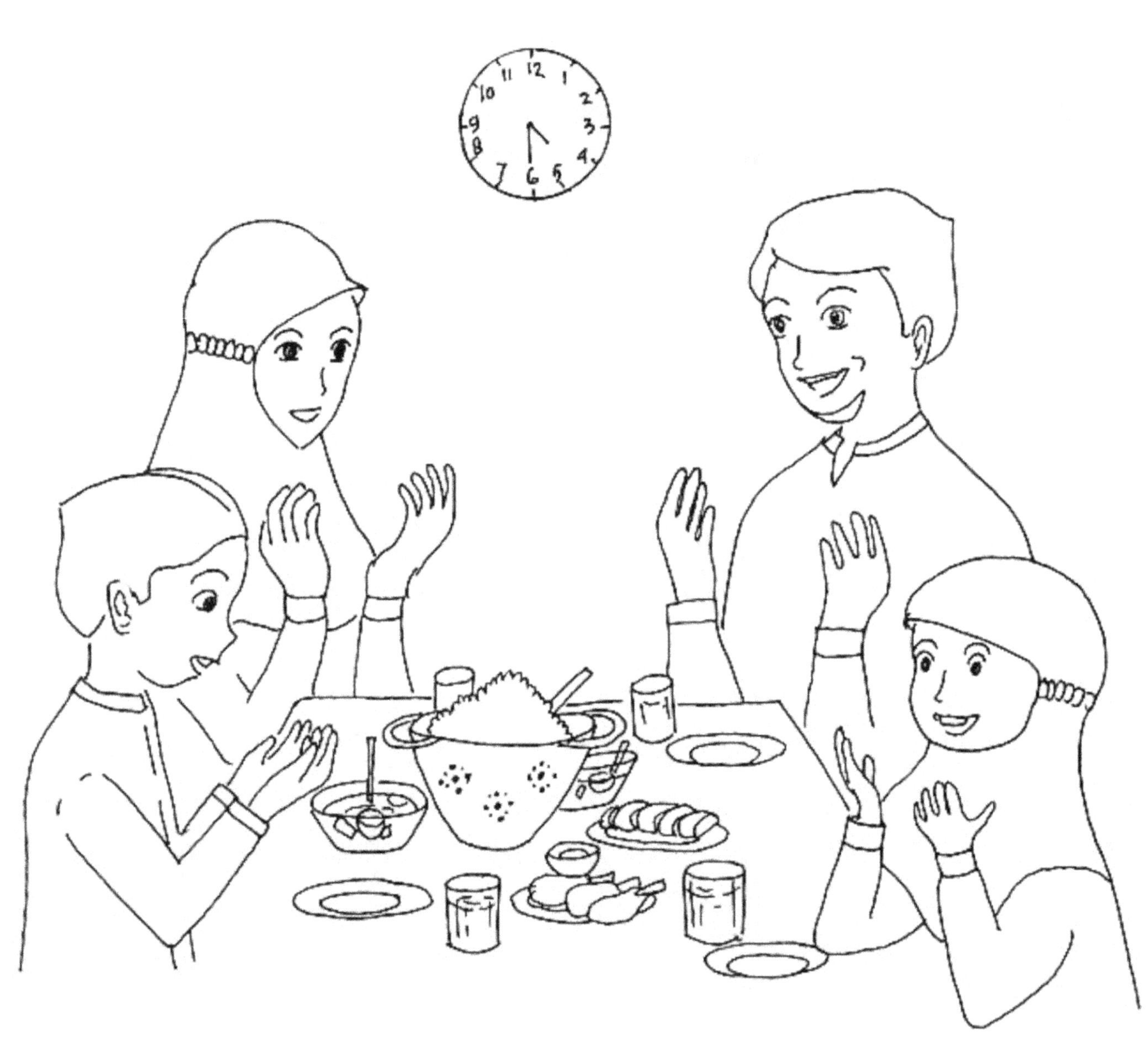

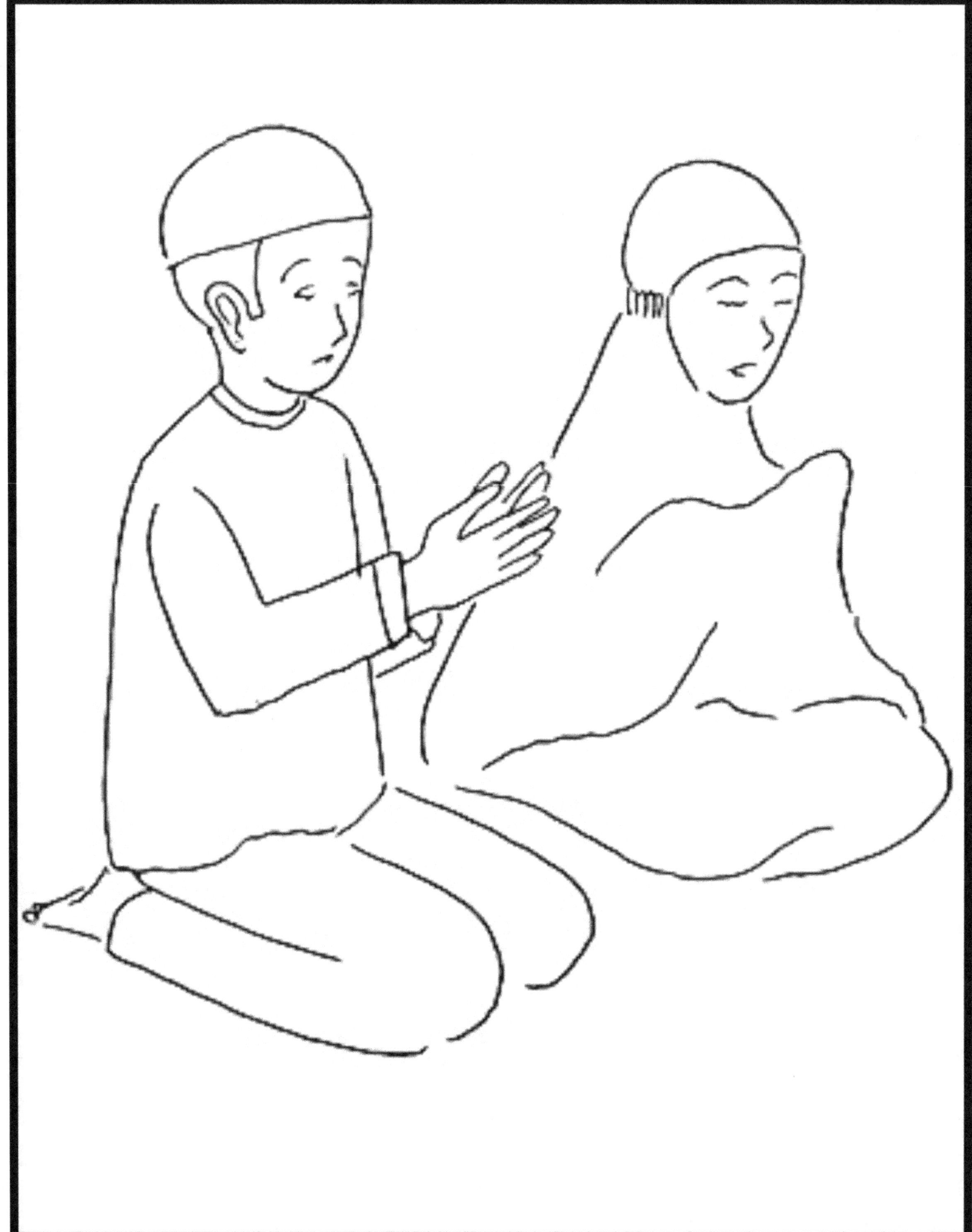

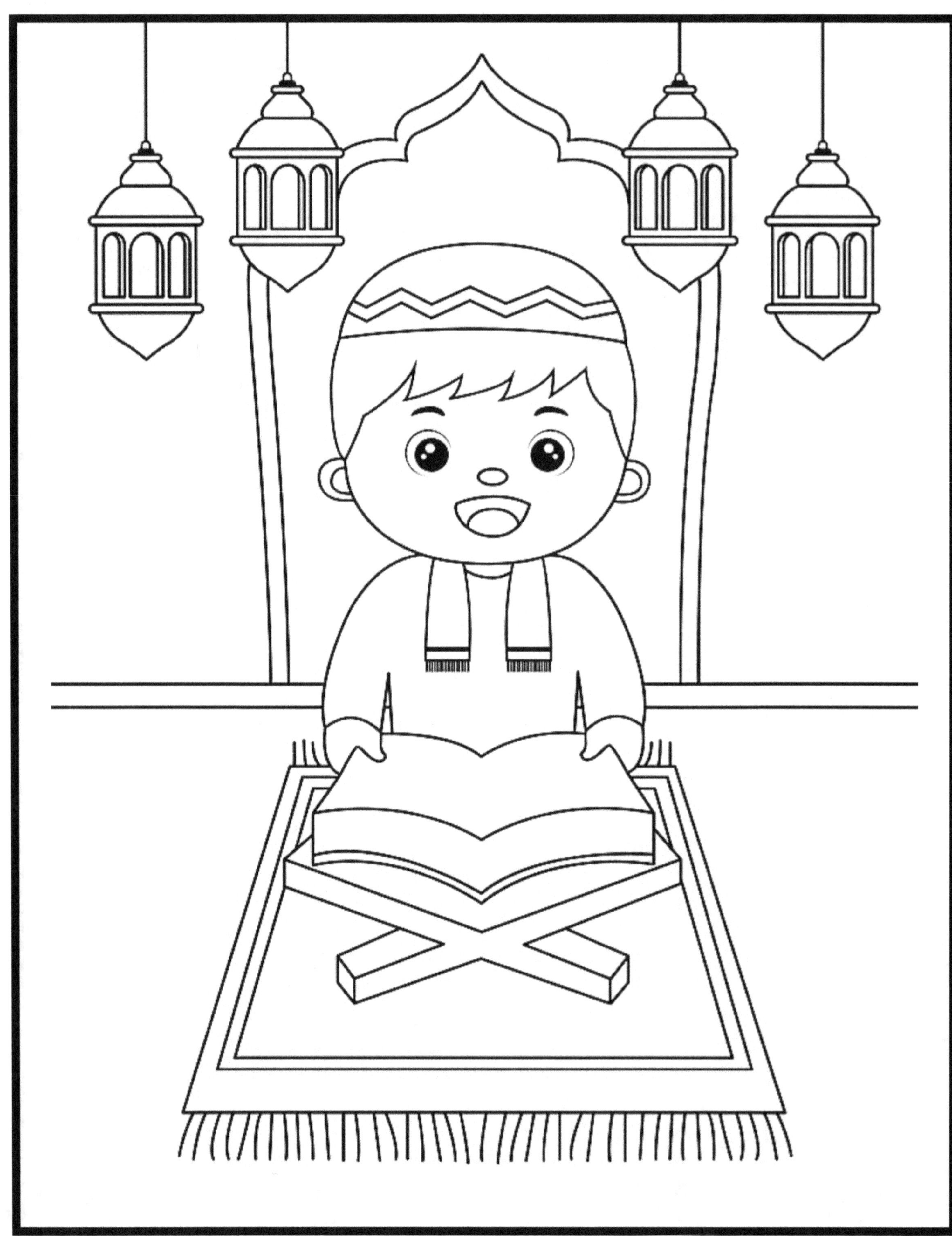

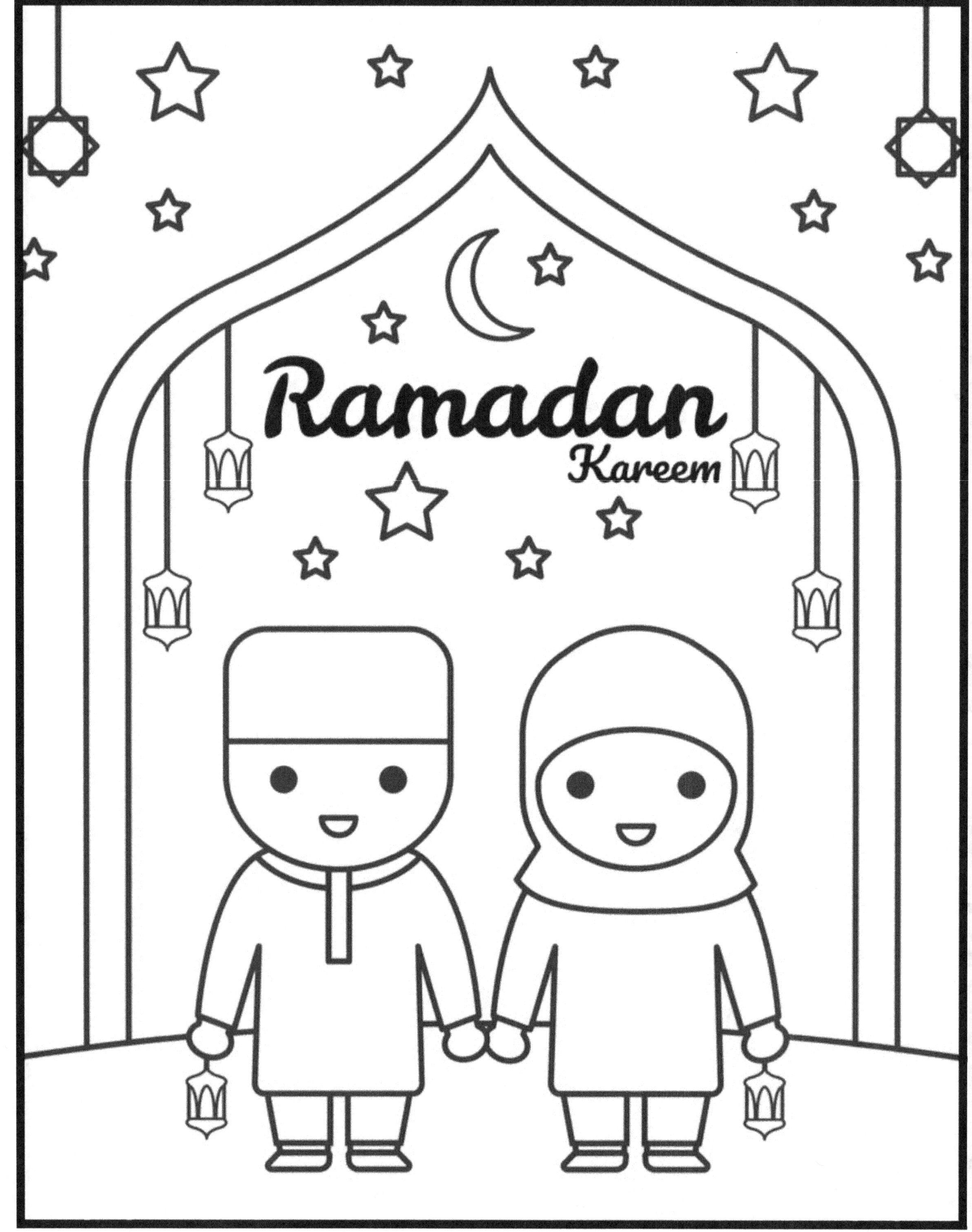

Ramadan
Kareem

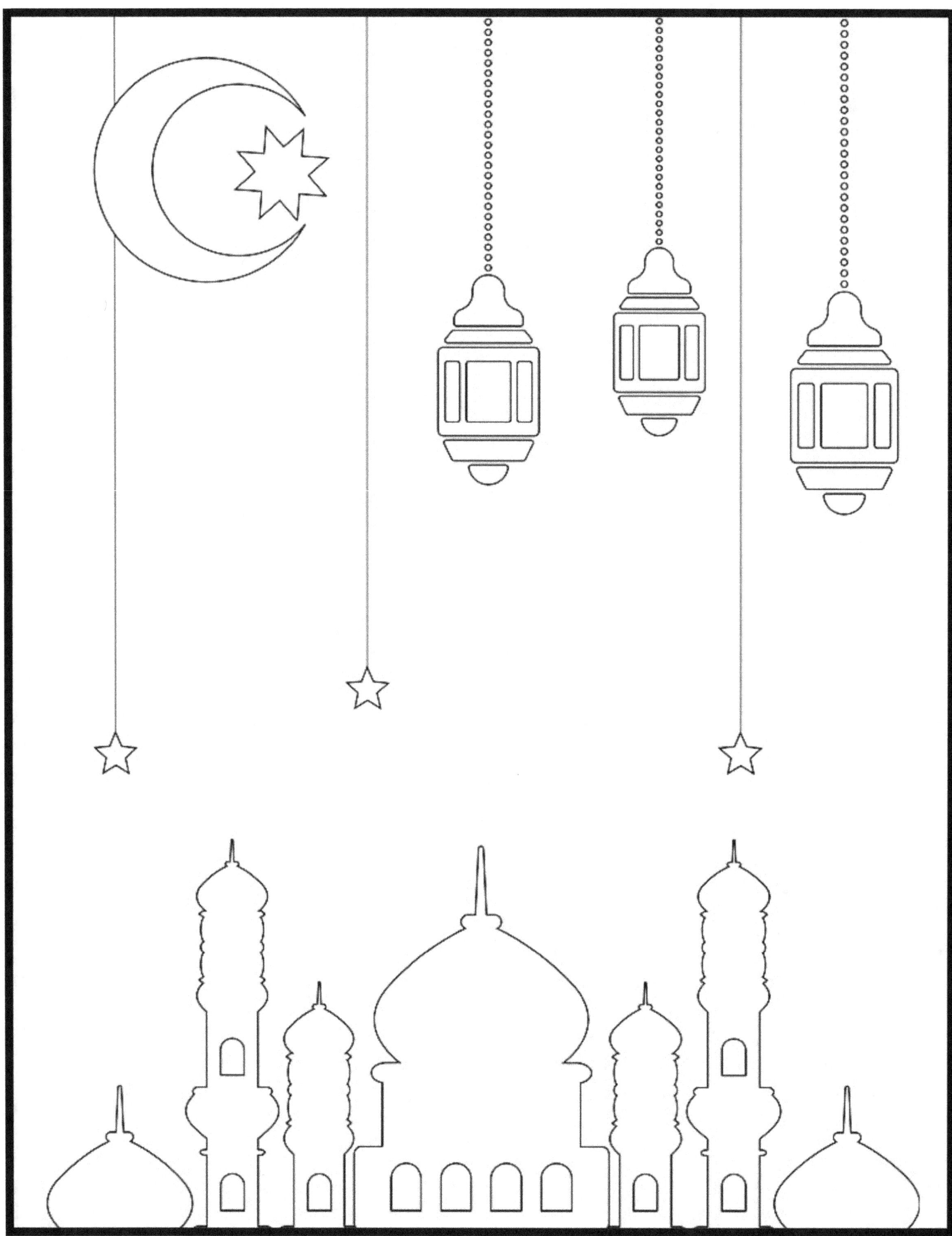

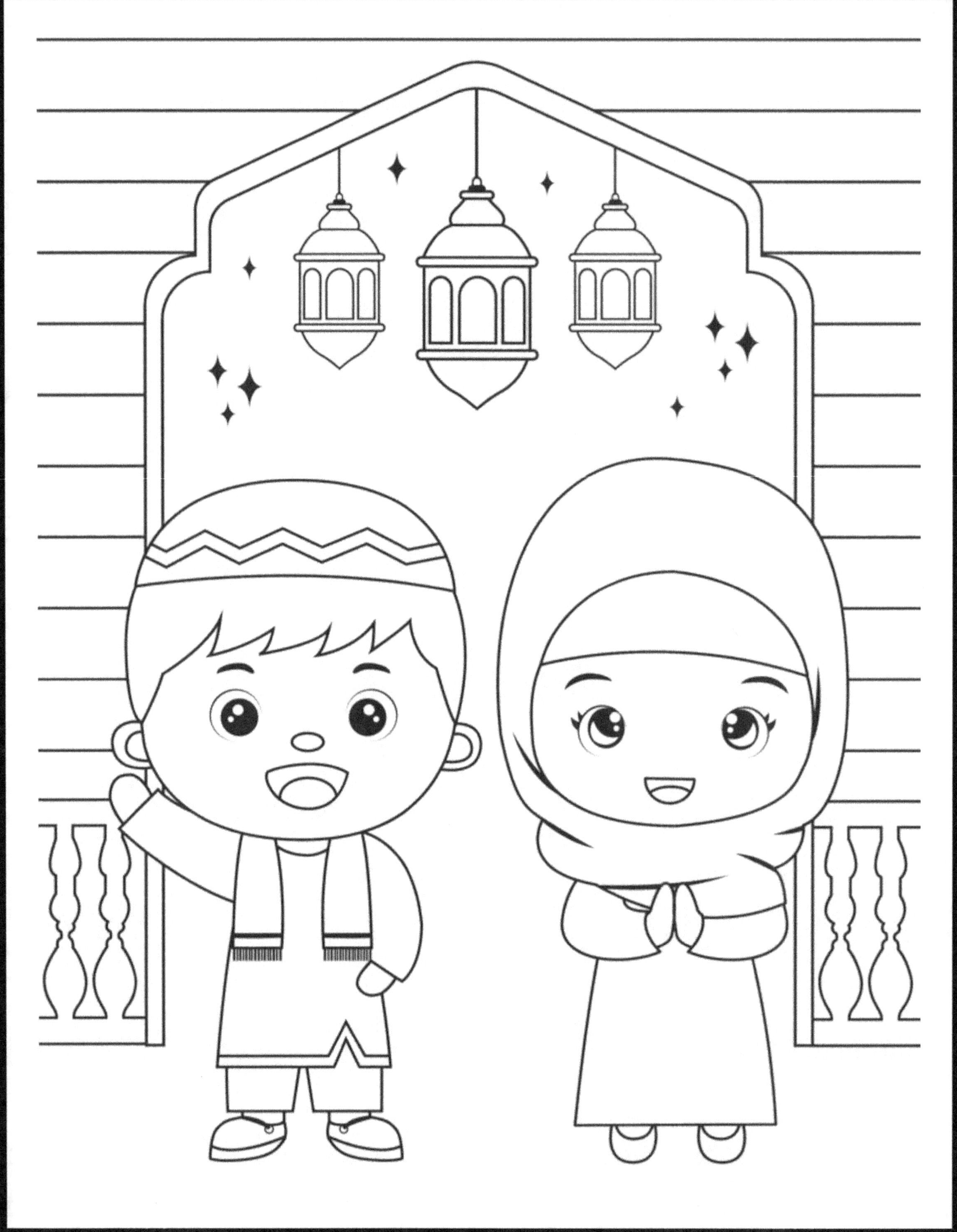

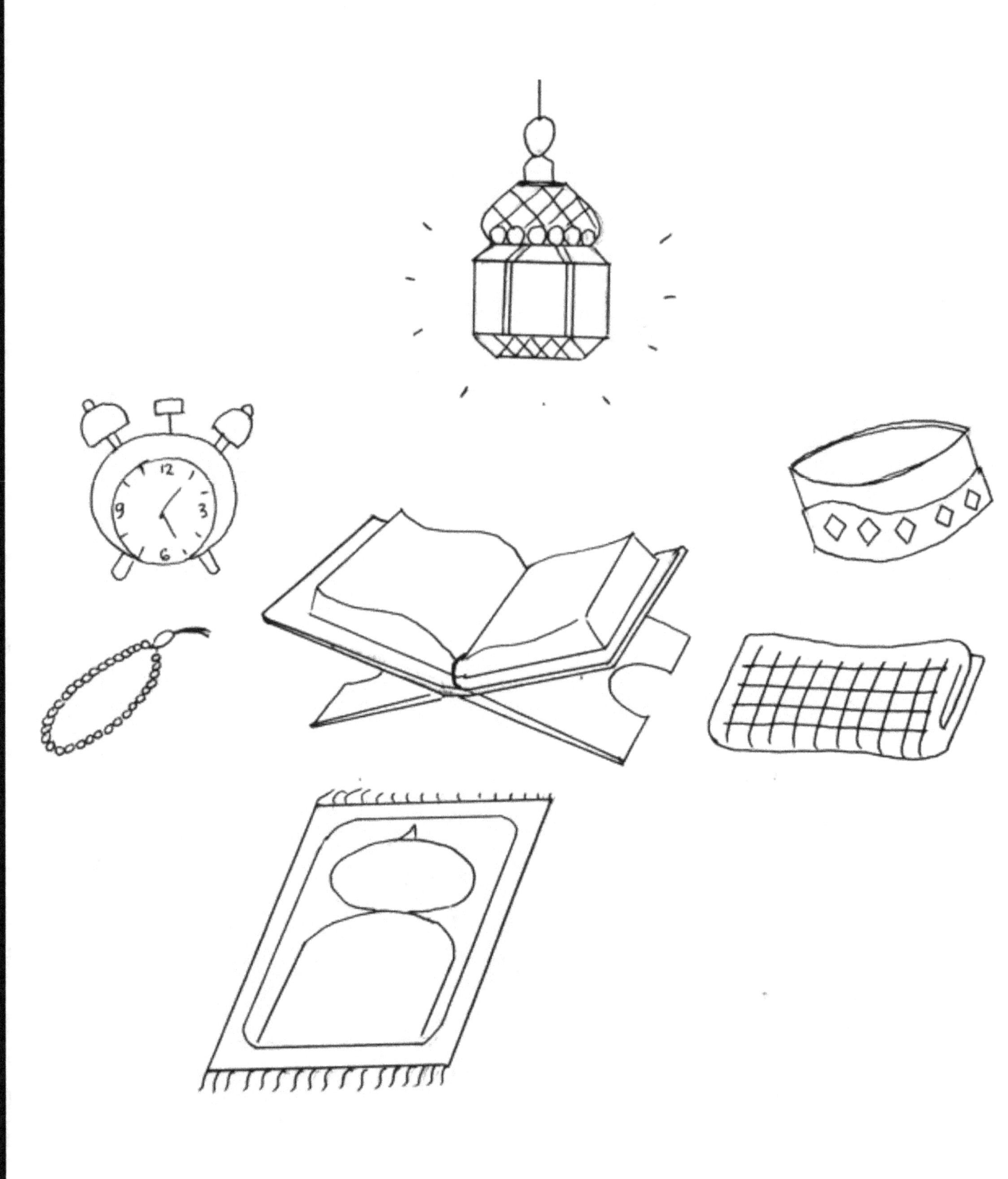

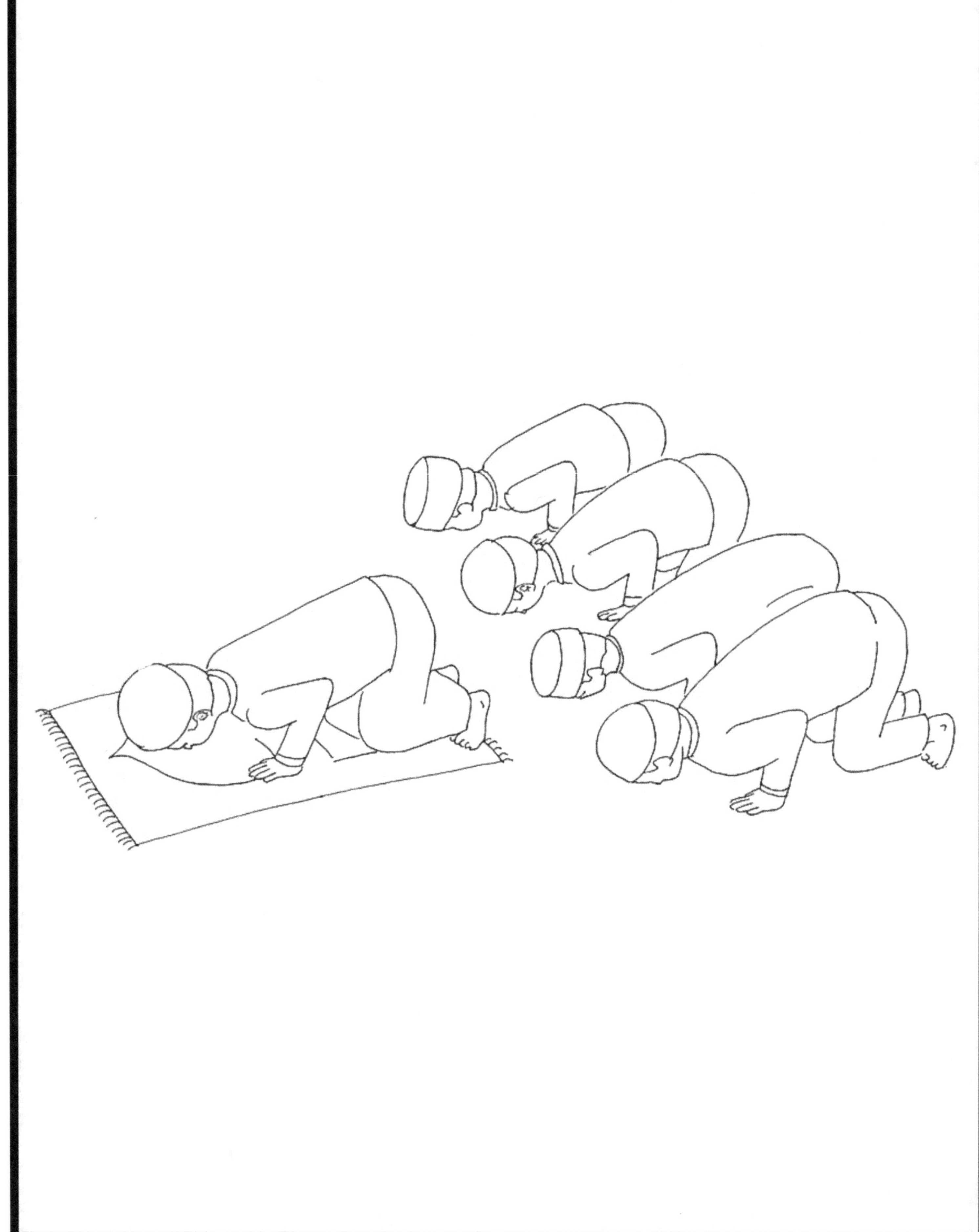

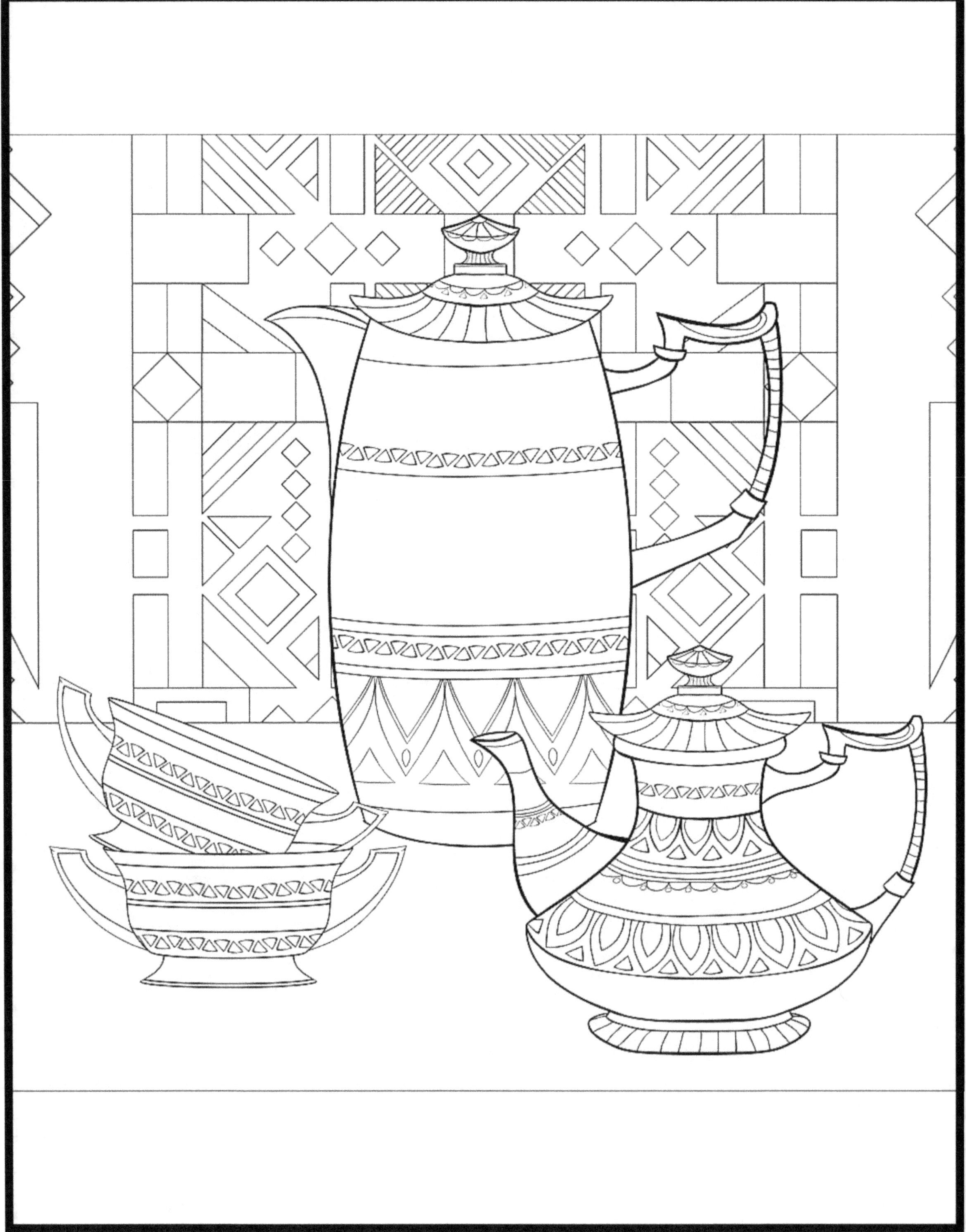

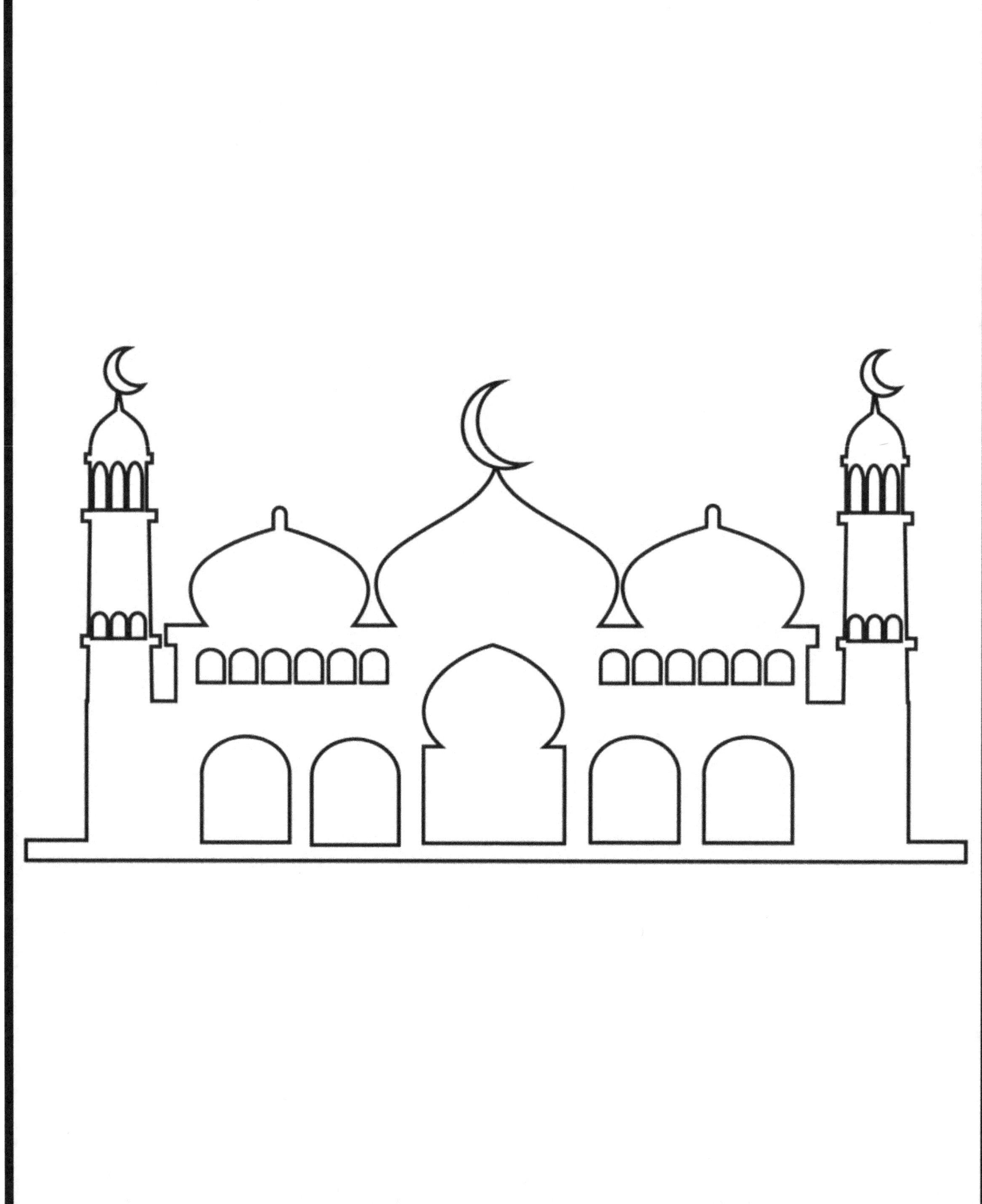

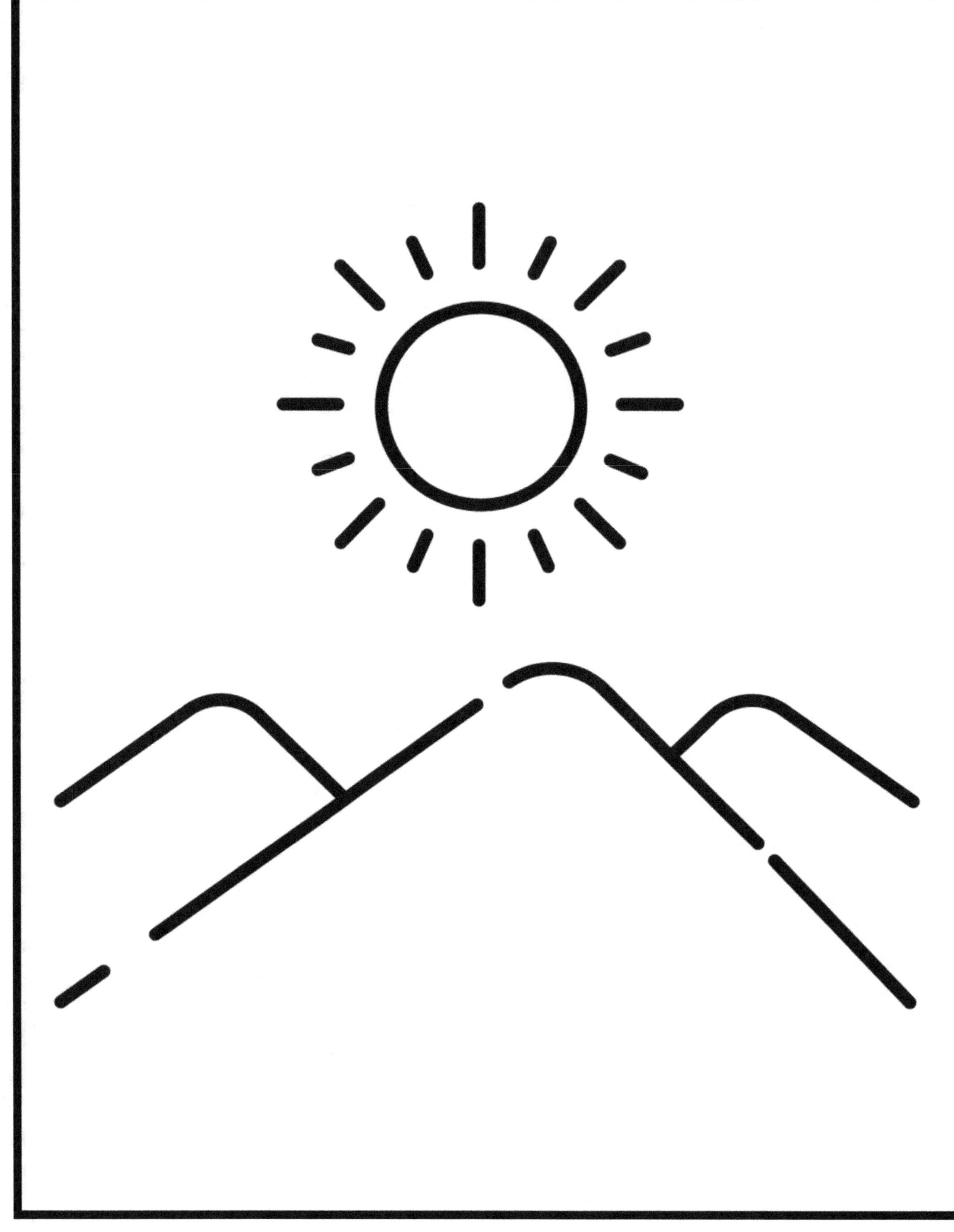

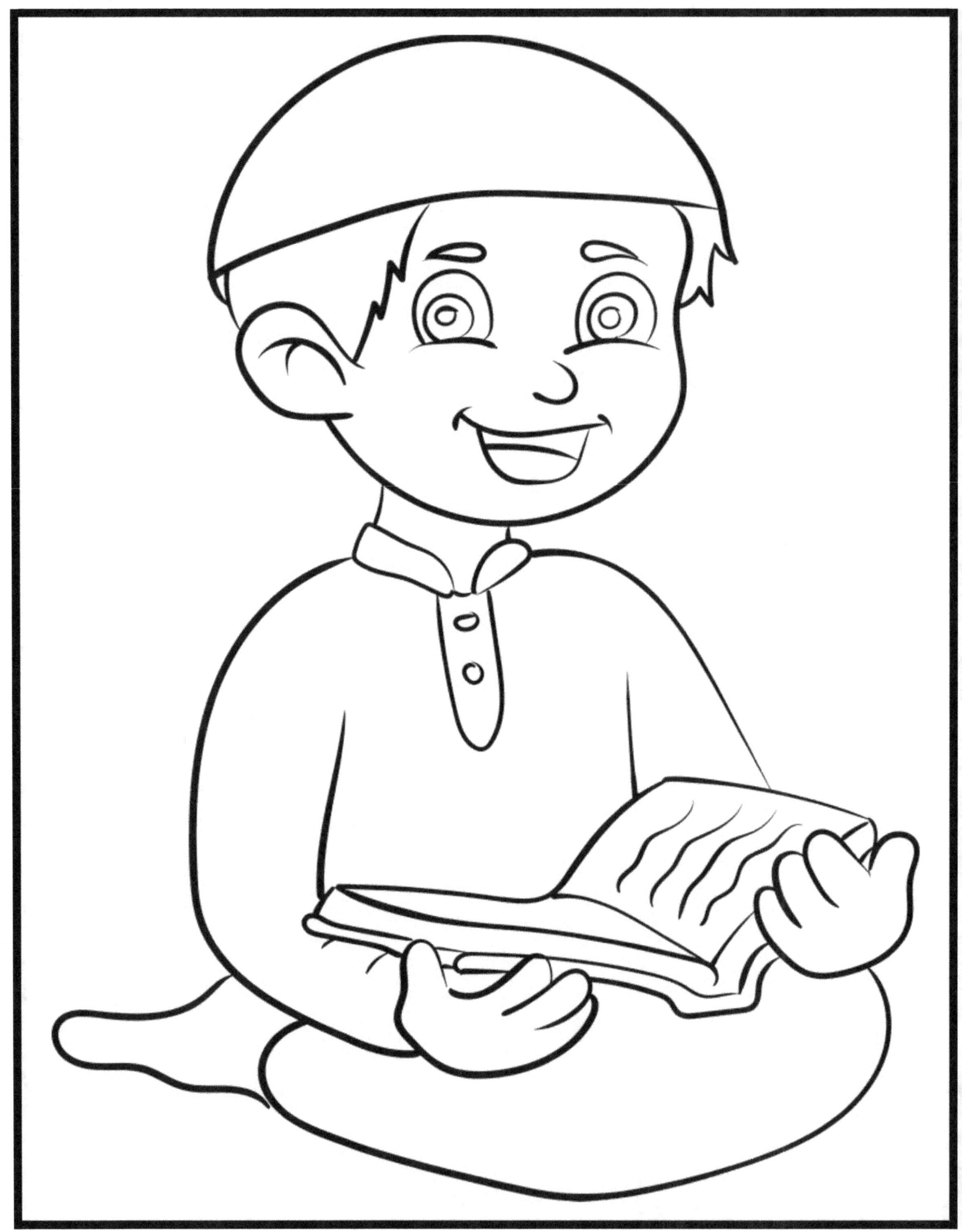

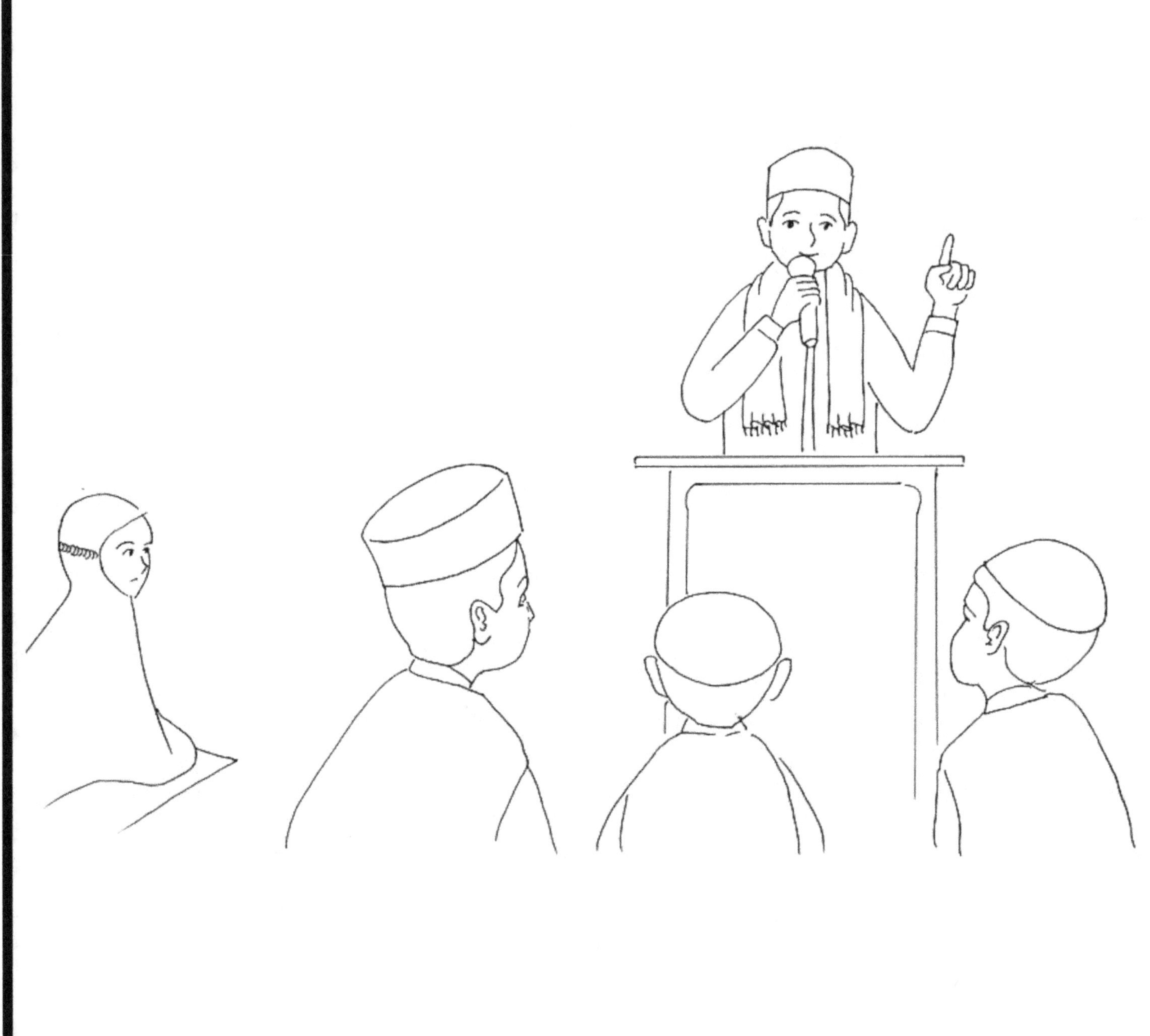

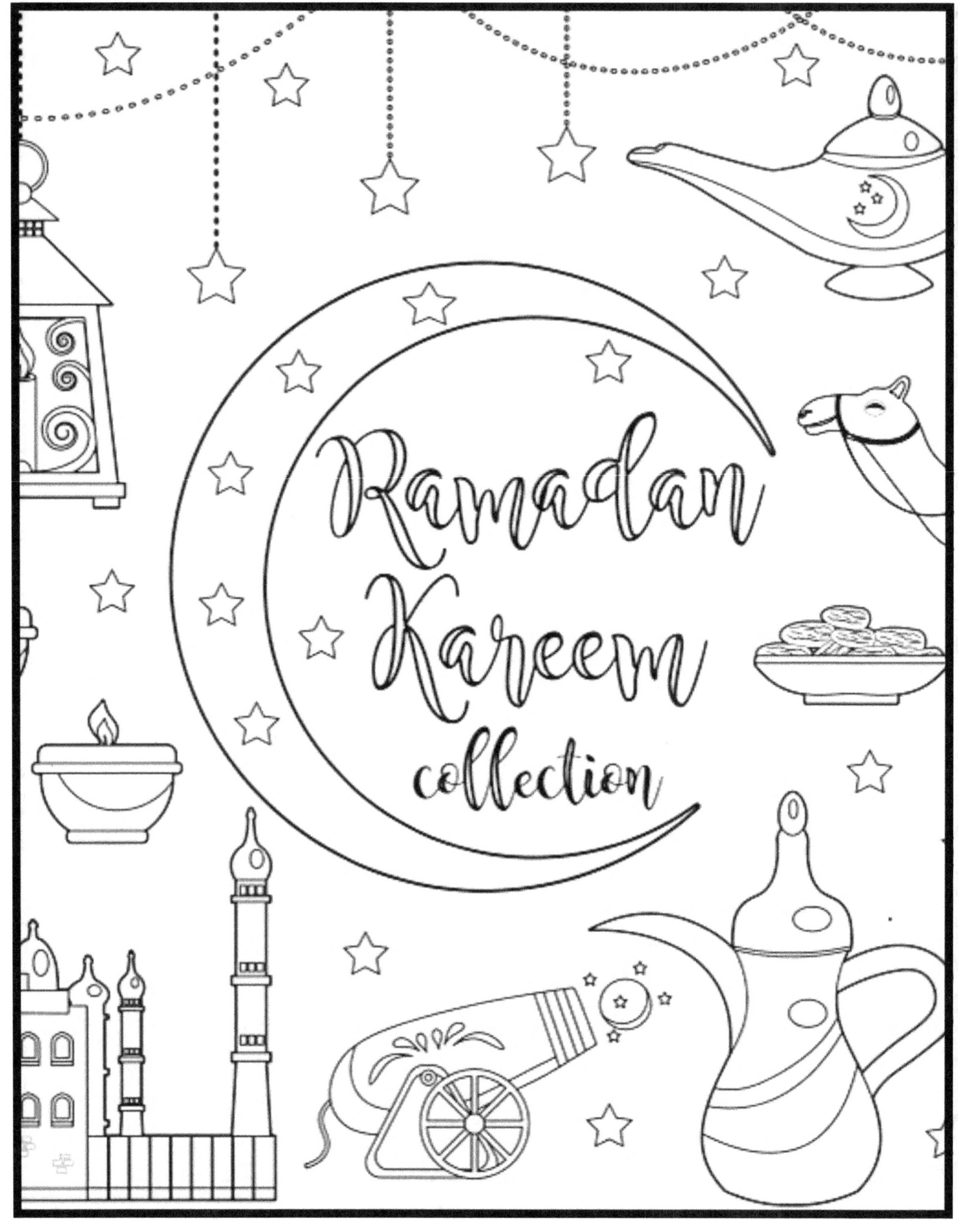
Ramadan
Kareem
collection

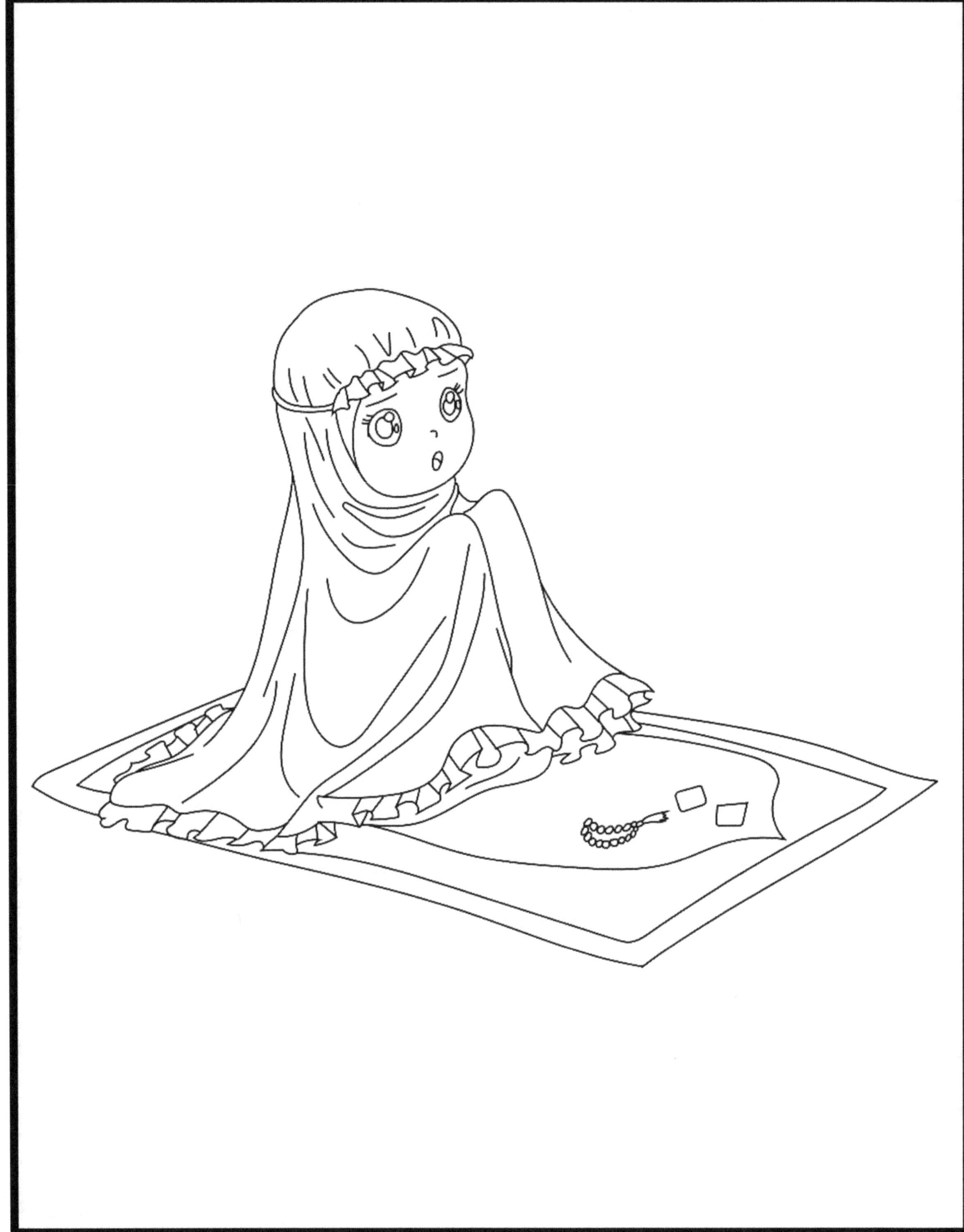

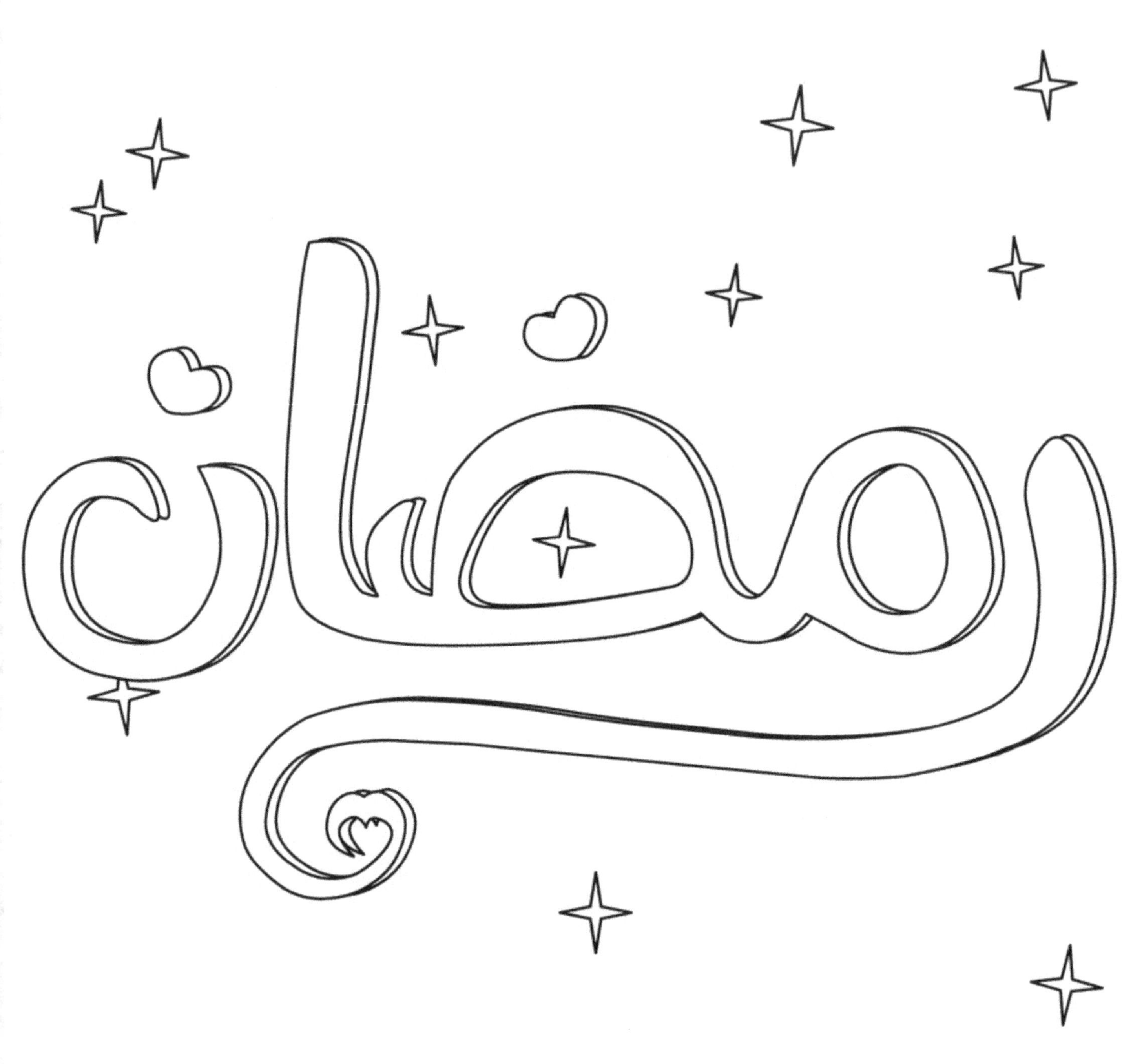

رمضان

Iftar

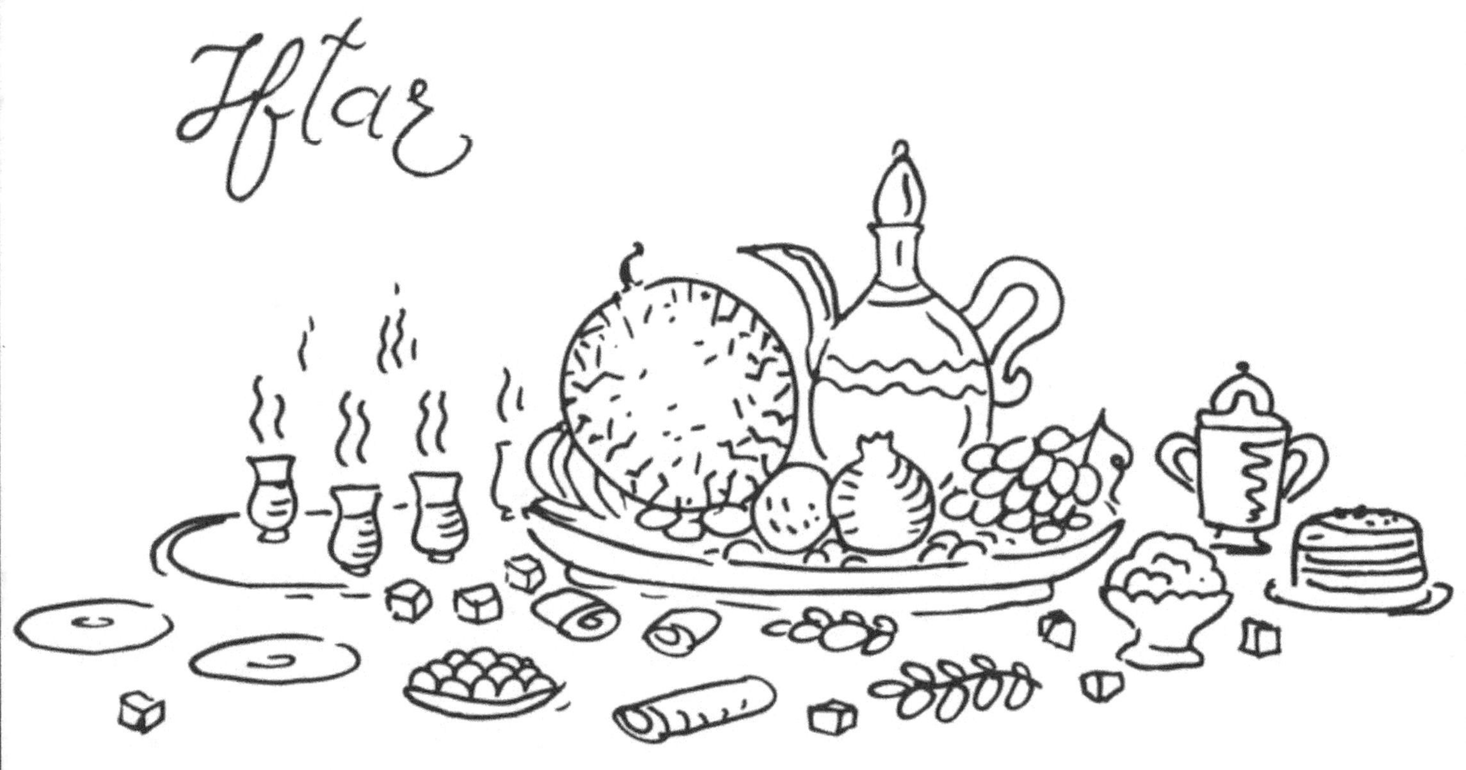

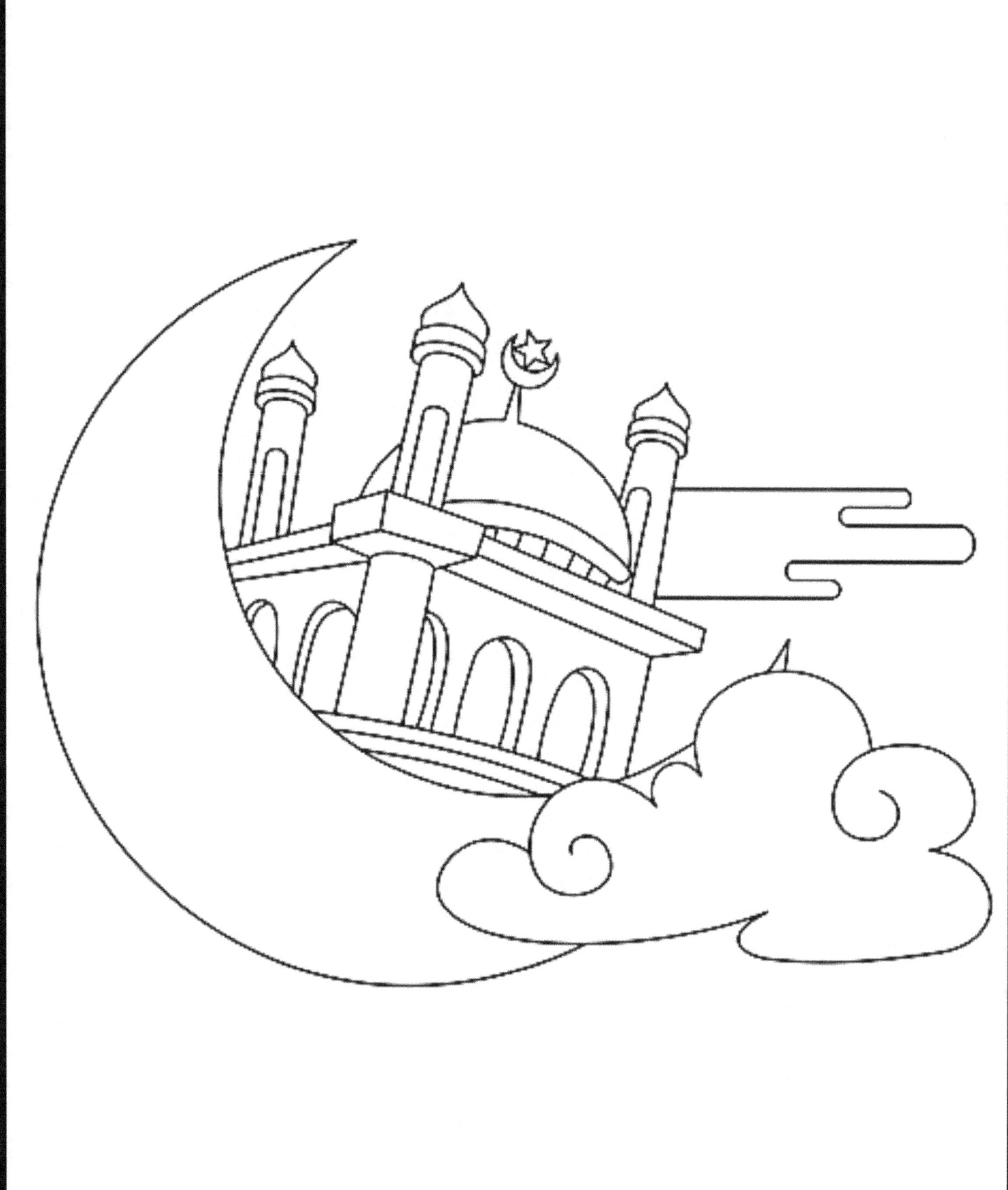

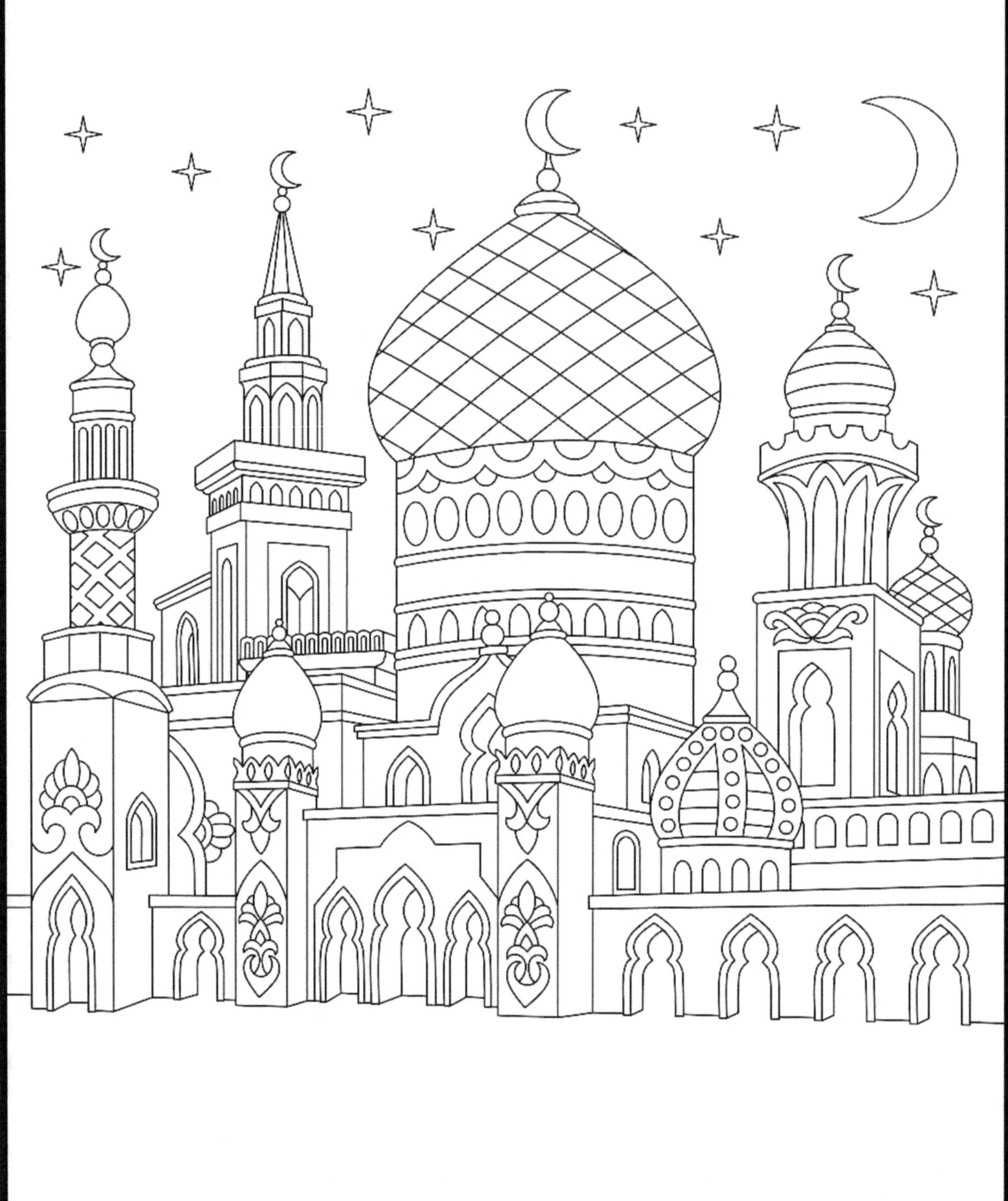

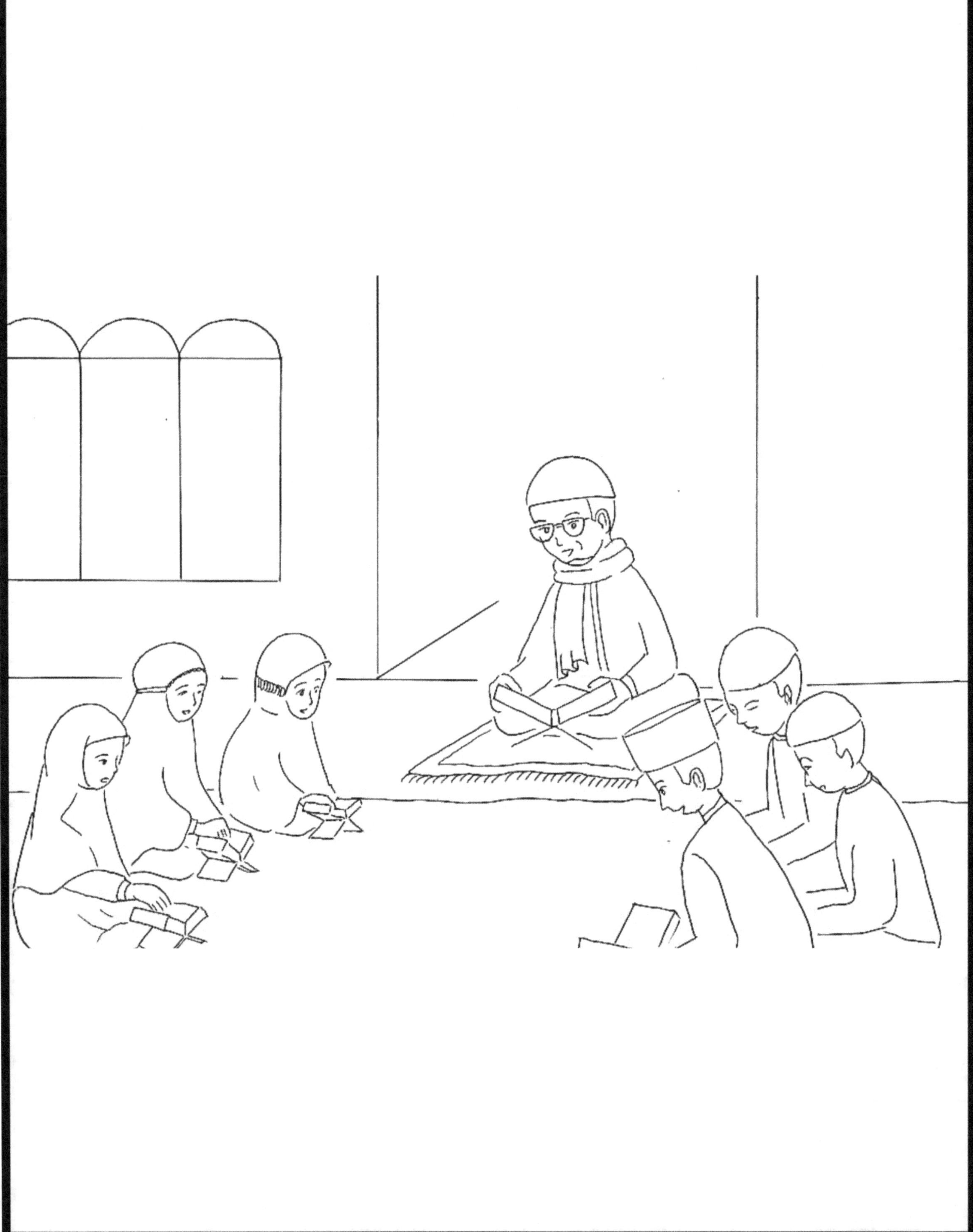

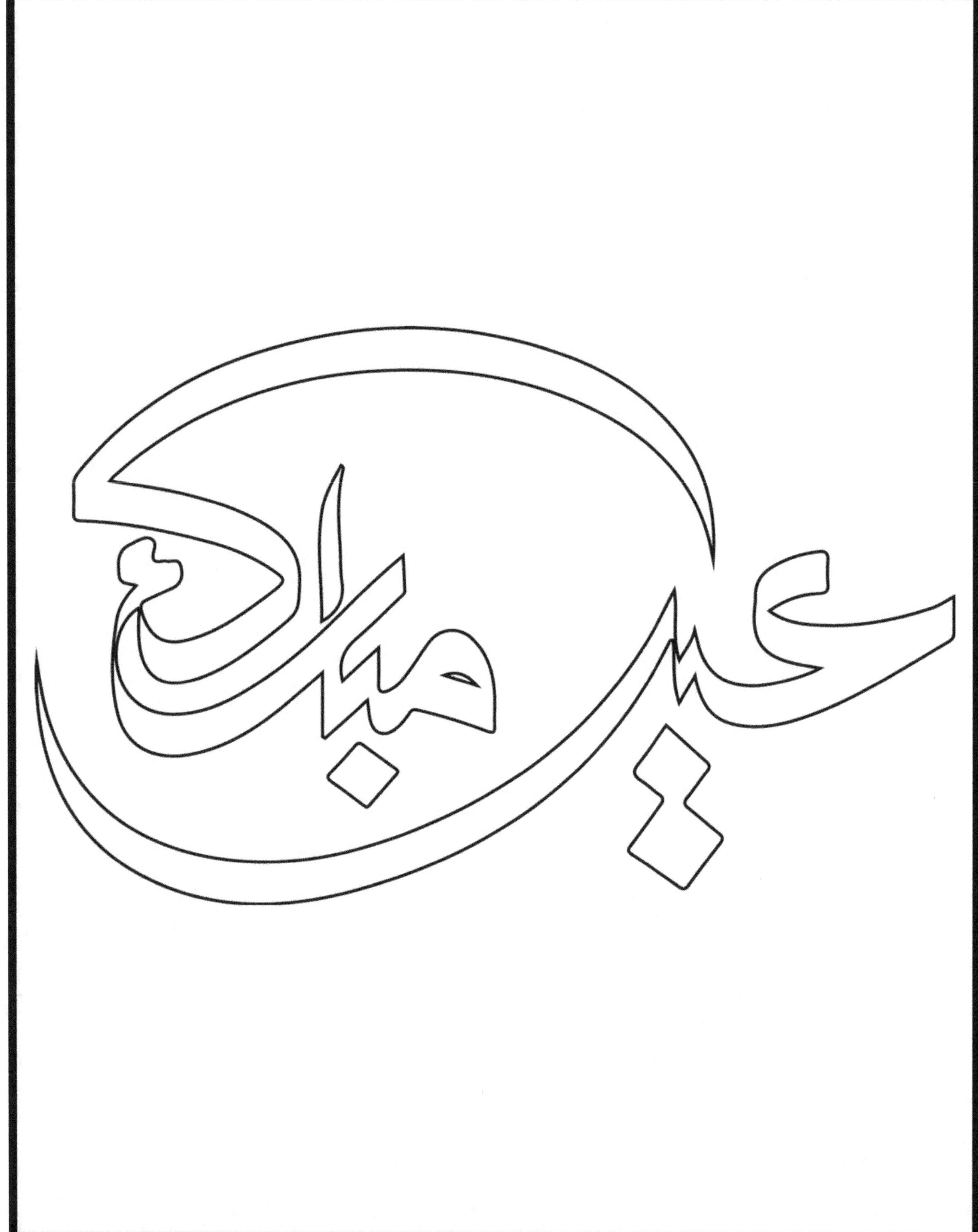
عيد مبارك

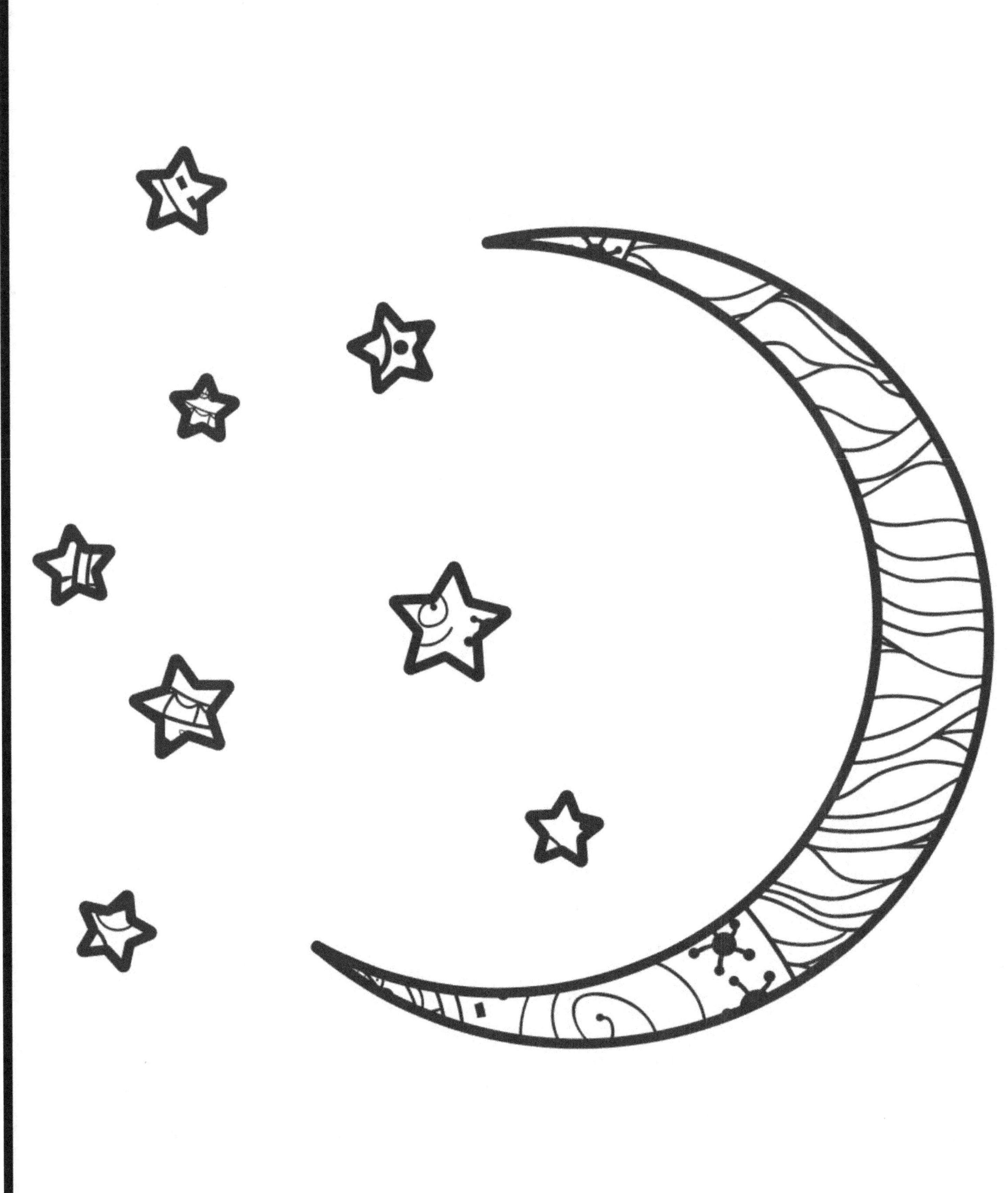

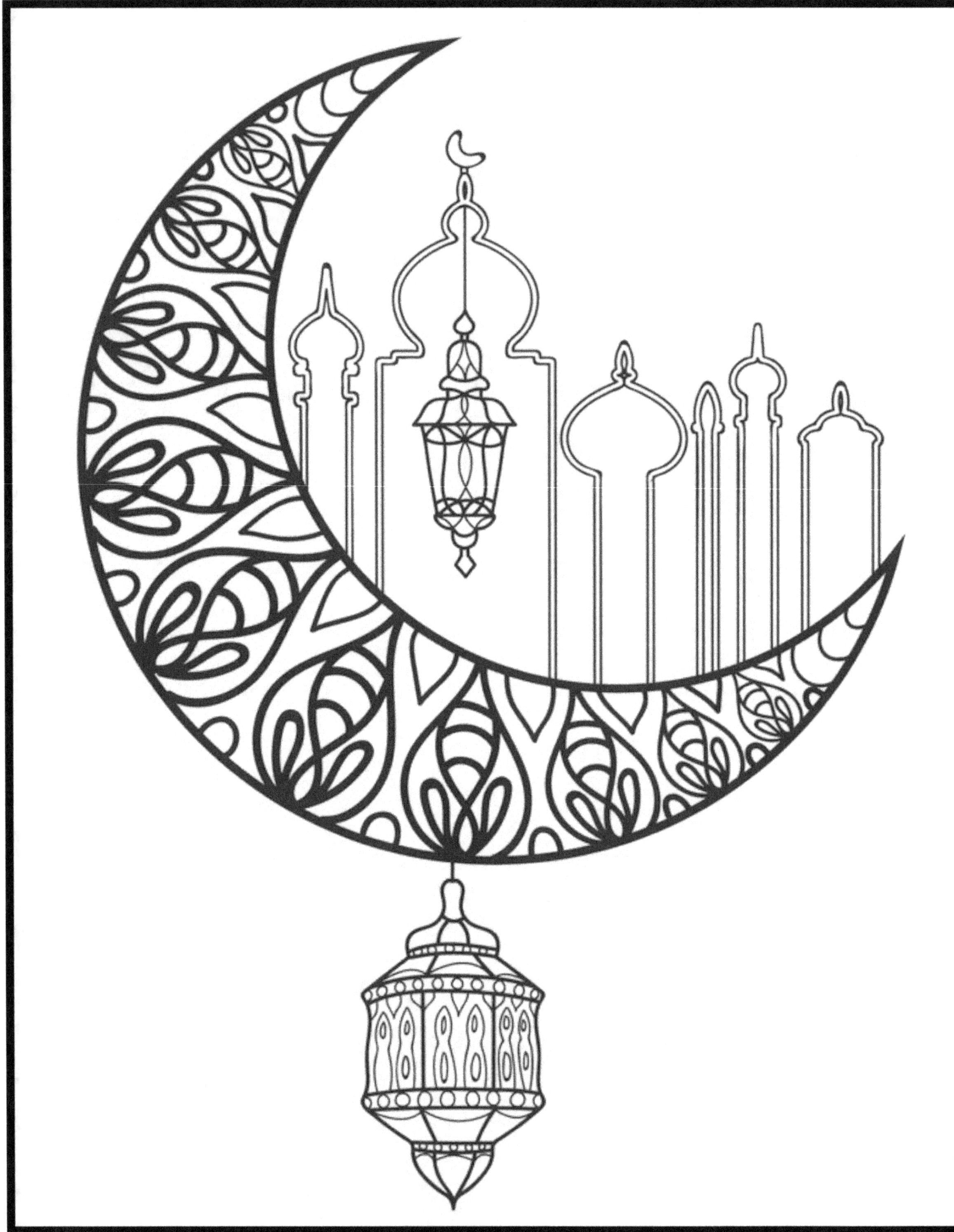

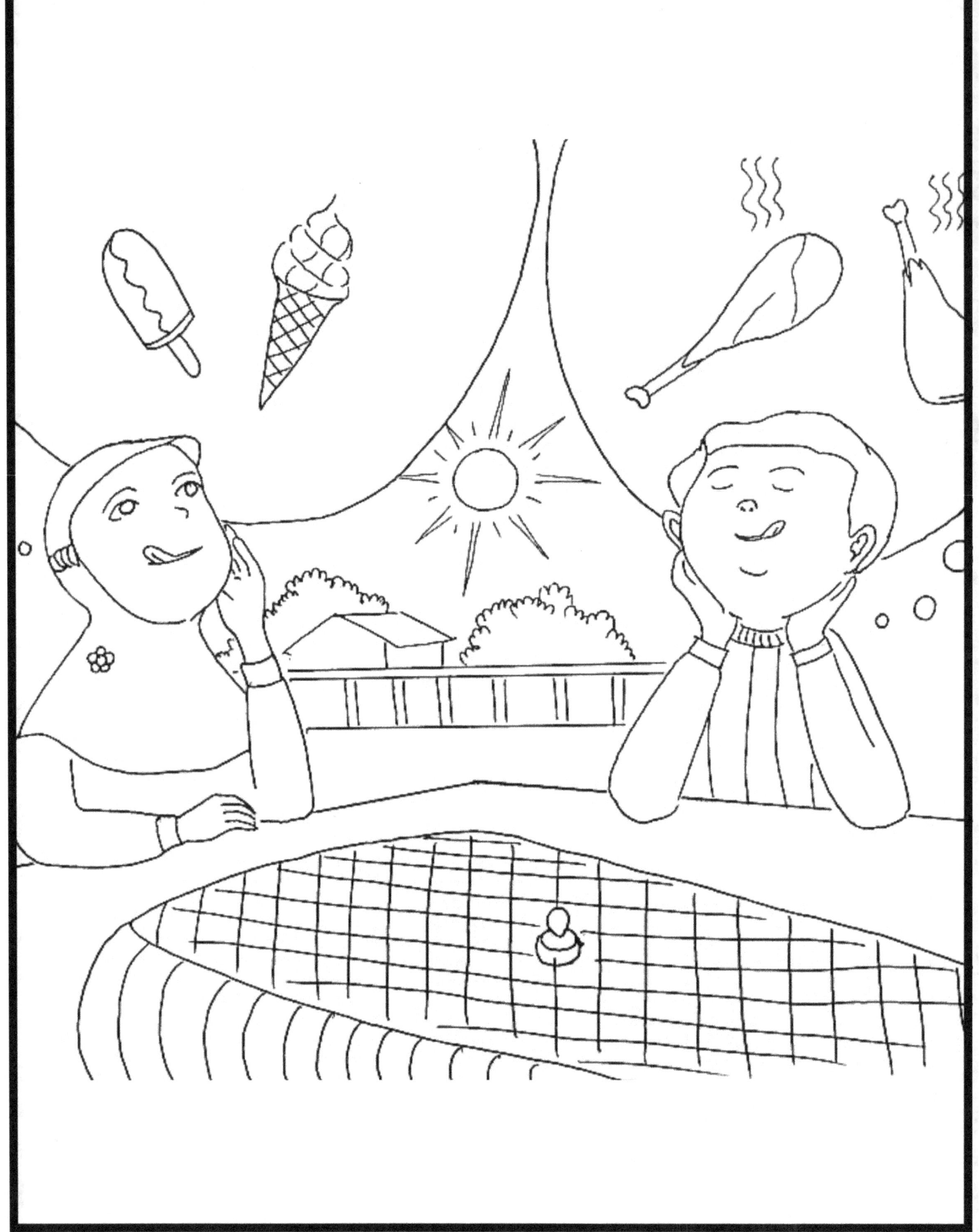

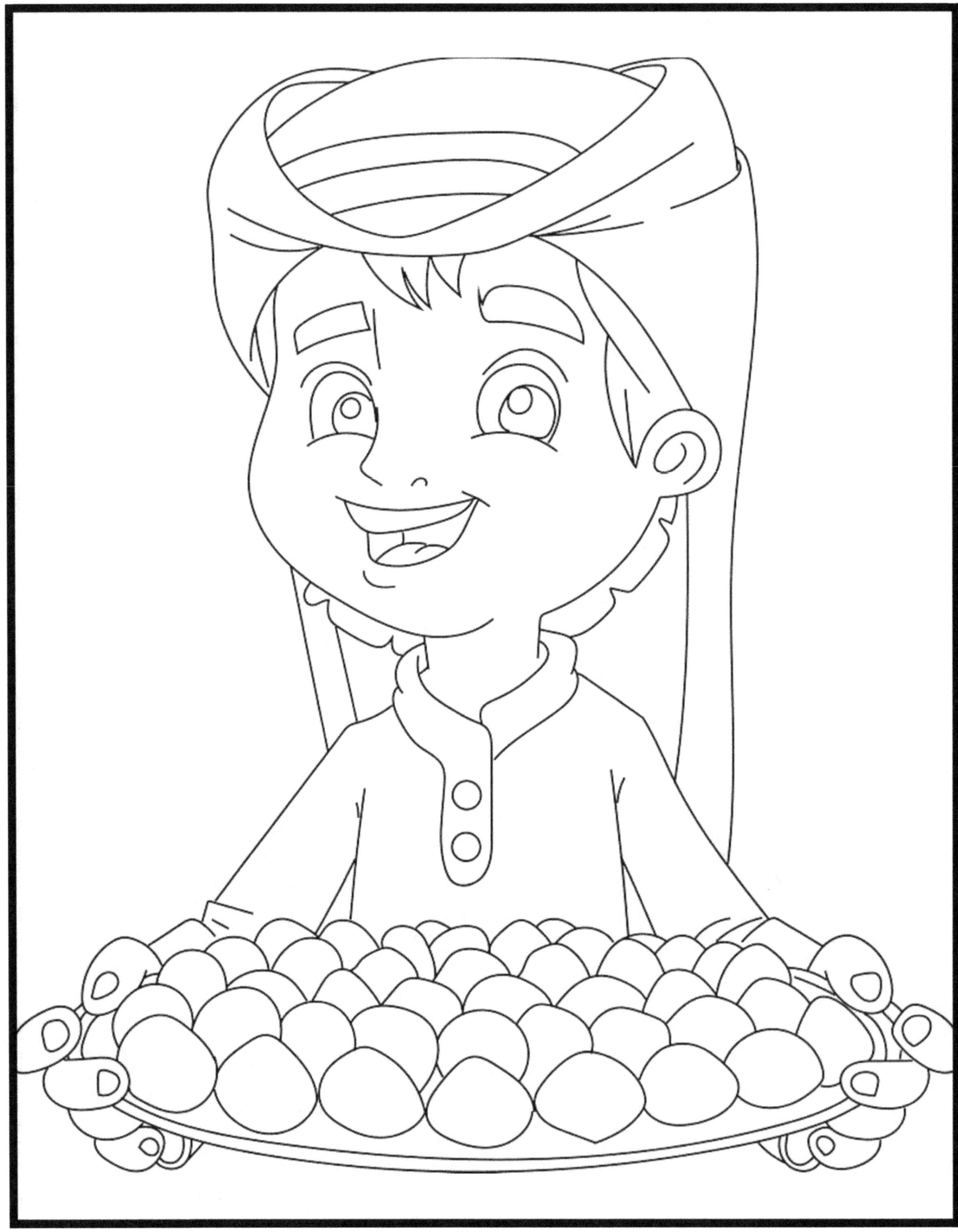

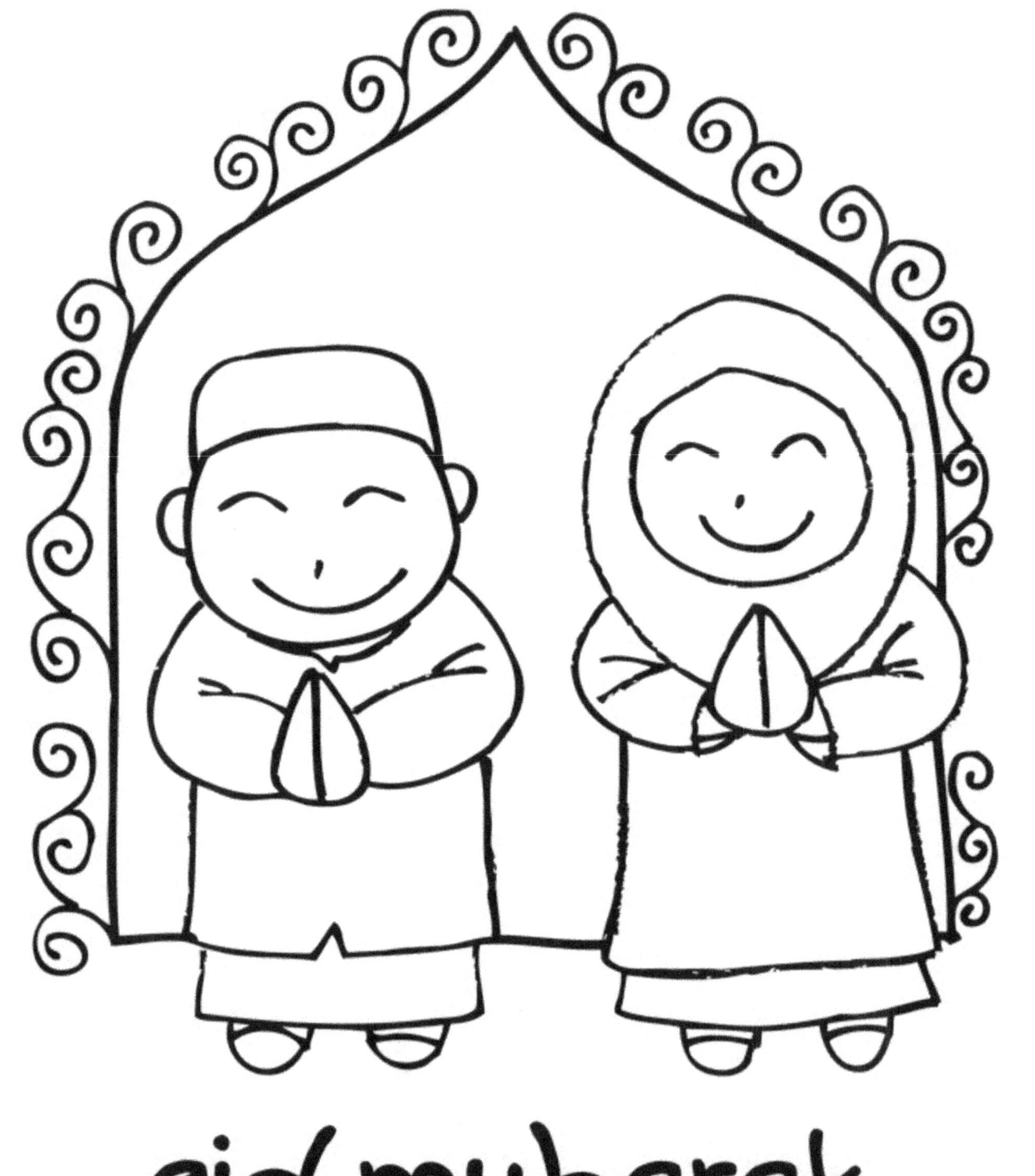

eid mubarak